ViVIeN
BOWeRS

CRIME SCENE

illustrated by

Martha Newbigging

MAPLE
TREE
PRESS

Maple Tree Press Inc.
51 Front Street East, Suite 200, Toronto, Ontario M5E 1B3
www.mapletreepress.com

Distributed in Canada by Raincoast Books
9050 Shaughnessy Street, Vancouver, British Columbia V6P 6E5

Distributed in the United States by Publishers Group West
1700 Fourth Street, Berkeley, California 94710

Cataloguing in Publication Data
Bowers, Vivien, 1951-
    Crime scene : how investigators use science to track down the bad guys / Vivien Bowers ; illustrated by Martha Newbigging.

Includes index.
Previously published under title: Crime science.
ISBN-13: 978-1-897066-55-3 (bound) / ISBN-10: 1-897066-55-4 (bound)
ISBN-13: 978-1-897066-56-0 (pbk.) / ISBN-10: 1-897066-56-2 (pbk.)

    1. Forensic sciences—Juvenile literature. 2. Criminal investigation —Juvenile literature. I. Newbigging, Martha II. Title.

HV8073.8.B68 2006   j363.25   C2005-904646-5

Design & art direction: Julia Naimska (interior), Claudia Dávila (cover)
Illustrations: Martha Newbigging

Photo Credits
Pages 8, 10, 15, 16, 20, 21, 22, Vancouver Forensic Laboratory; 9, 12, 47 (top), R.C.M.P., Nelson Subdivision; 11, 49, Dr. David Sweet, University of British Columbia; 24, UPI/Corbis-Bettmann; 29 (top), Robert Willet/Raleigh News Observer/Sygma, (bottom) Jim Bounds/Raleigh News Observer/Sygma; 32–33, Kim Rossmo/Vancouver Police Department; 36 (top), 50, Cam Pye/R.C.M.P. "E" Division Artist H.Q.; 43, R.C.M.P. Central Forensic Laboratory, Ottawa; 47 (bottom), Dr. Mark Skinner/Simon Fraser University; 51, Vancouver Sun; 52, Bill Ivy; 54, L.A. Josza/Forintek Canada; 55, Rolf Mathewes/Simon Fraser University; cover, Matthias Kulka/CORBIS. Every attempt has been made to contact the owners of copyright for the images used in *Crime Scene*.

We acknowledge the financial support of the Canada Council for the Arts, the Ontario Arts Council, the Government of Canada through the Book Publishing Industry Development Program (BPIDP), and the Government of Ontario through the Ontario Media Development Corporation's Book Initiative for our publishing activities.

ONTARIO ARTS COUNCIL
CONSEIL DES ARTS DE L'ONTARIO

Printed in China

A   B   C   D   E   F

ConteNts

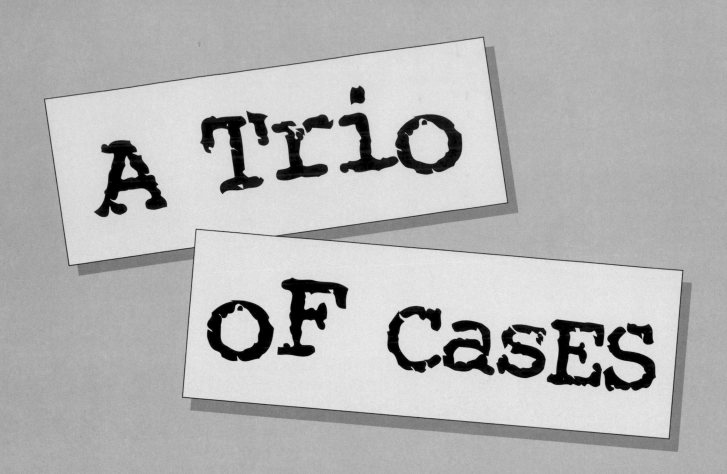

A Trio of CasES

Ever wondered if you'd make a good investigator? Crime sleuths need to be smart, patient and determined. The clues are out there. So crime investigators search crime scenes bit by bit for evidence to send back to the lab. In the lab, forensic scientists probe the evidence. They magnify it, run it through machines, separate it into parts and shine lasers on it. They search for information that fits together, like pieces of a puzzle, until the truth comes out.

This book takes you to the scene of the crime, to the crime lab and into the heads of investigators. You'll get a chance to hone your sleuthing skills with Clue Ins. You'll find Case Files describing how police solve crimes and catch criminals: some as real as the latest police report, some made up of details from several cases. Ready to tackle some criminals? Let's head for the scene of the crime!

One, Two, Three, Forensic

You'll come across the word "forensic" a lot in this book. You'll read about forensic chemists, forensic dentists and all sorts of other forensic experts. The "forensic" part means that these people use their special knowledge and skills to help solve crimes.

AT THE SCENE OF THE CRIME

It's a busy afternoon for the police in Anytown -- three different crimes, three separate investigations. Let's see what they're up to . . .

The Case of the Smoking Thief

10:35 a.m. — Anytown Bank
A white male wearing a brown jacket tried to cash a check. When the teller identified the check as counterfeit and refused, the crook drew a gun and demanded money. A customer screamed, so the man fired a shot into the air and told everyone to shut up. He reached over and grabbed a stack of bills from the teller, then escaped from the bank with more than $10,000.

Police arrived and closed off the bank. They took statements from witnesses, including one who saw the thief smoke a cigarette and drop the butt on the ground before entering the bank. A police artist is using witness descriptions to draw a sketch of the thief. Evidence includes the cigarette butt, the fake check, the bullet dug out of the bank's ceiling and some brown fibers found wedged in a crack in the teller's window. These clues were sent to the crime lab for analysis.

The Case of the Cyberspace Crook

11:00 a.m. — Anytown College A paleontology professor just logged in to her computer and found her most important files were gone! In Mongolia a few months ago, she found fossils of a never-before documented dinosaur. As the first person to publish information about it, the professor would "scoop" paleontologists all over the world.

The police think the thief was able to access the professor's files remotely (from some-where else). So there's no point in searching the office for evidence. How do you find a robber in cyberspace?

The Case of the Mysterious Bones

4:45 p.m. — Outskirts of Anytown Police got a call from kids who found some bones while playing in the woods. When study of the bones proved they were human, it really shocked the kids, but it got police investigators right on the case.

The police used yellow tape to close off the area. The whole place was crawling with investigators wearing "bunny suits" to prevent them from leaving their own traces at the scene. They took photographs and recorded the location of everything on a scale drawing. The area was searched, and each piece of evidence was picked up with tweezers and put in its own plastic bag.

The evidence, including dirt from the scene and some white bugs found with the bones, went to the crime lab. The bones went to the morgue. Examination of everything can reveal who the person was, how the death occurred and why the body was in the woods.

Three mysteries for the Anytown police and their forensic experts. By the time you've finished this book, you'll know enough about forensic science to understand how each of these cases could be solved. (See page 61, but try to solve the crimes yourself as you read along . . .)

Match-ing up Evidence

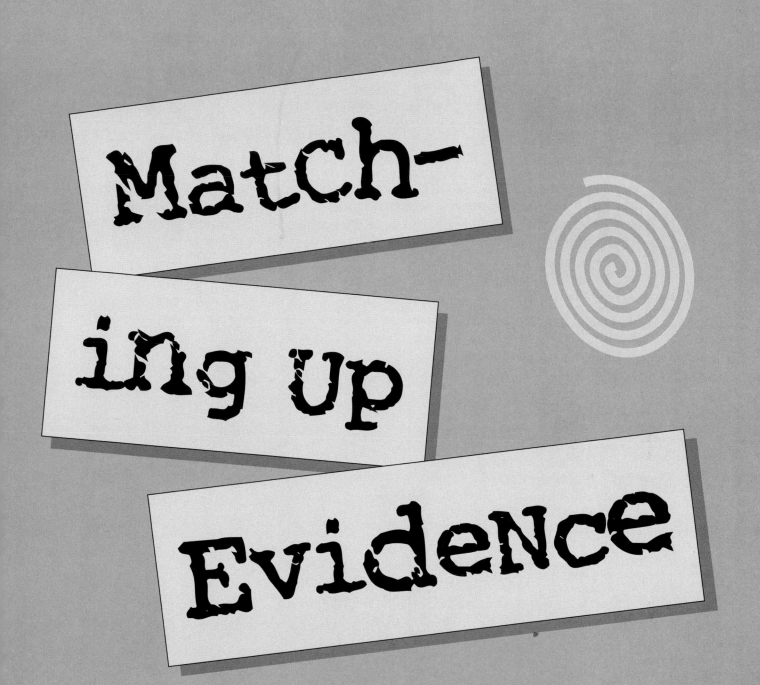

Would you believe a broken pistachio nut could be a key piece of evidence to a murder? It was found in the rolled-up cuff of pants worn by a suspect, and perfectly matched one of the bits of shell found at the scene of the crime. The murderer walked off with evidence that connected him to the crime. Snacking can be dangerous!

It's a Match

Solving a crime is like doing a jigsaw puzzle — you fit the pieces together to get the whole picture. Sometimes those puzzle pieces are very small. Many investigations involve matching a tiny piece of evidence with its source — wherever it might have come from. It's one way to link a criminal to a crime scene . . . and a crime.

A Perfect Fit

Criminals usually take away a trace of the crime scene or leave something behind, no matter how careful they are. It can be something so small it's barely noticeable — one strand of hair stuck to clothing, a tiny scrape on a windowsill where a crowbar was used to pry the window open. Police link a suspect to a crime scene by proving that two objects — one from the suspect and one from the crime scene — were once attached to each other. With evidence, as with pieces of a jigsaw puzzle, they look at where the pieces fit together.

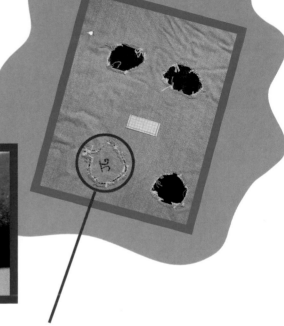

Electrical wires were snipped when a car radio was stolen. The cut end of one of the wires in the car matches a wire on a radio found in a suspect's car trunk.

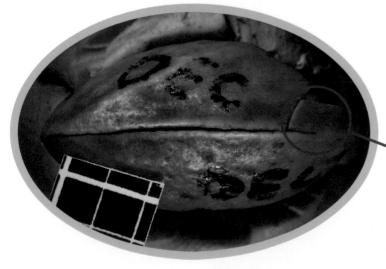

This hold-up mask was left behind at the scene of a robbery. Circles of blue cloth found in a garbage can in the suspect's apartment perfectly matched the eye holes. (Why are there four eye holes? That mystery hasn't been solved.)

This broken piece of pistachio nut, found in a murder suspect's pants cuff, perfectly matches one of the pieces found on the floor at the murder scene. Once something becomes evidence, the police have to measure and label it very carefully. Note the grid to show the size, and the writing on the pistachio shell.

"Ax"-ing Questions

The police weren't sure what to expect when they were called out to the school. Thieves had broken into the principal's office looking for money. What a mess! Drawers were pulled out, papers were all over the floor, and a metal safe was broken open and tipped upside down.

While carefully looking for clues, an investigator found a tiny sliver of wood lying on the floor near the safe. She checked the office furniture, but nothing was made of the same wood. There wasn't anything there the sliver could have come from. What if it had broken off the tool used to force open the safe? From the marks on the safe, it looked like the thief had used an ax.

Soon police had a suspect. They searched his home and found an ax with a broken handle behind the house. Hardly visible to the naked eye was a small nick in the handle. Would it match the sliver of wood they had found on the floor of the principal's office? Under the microscope, the two pieces fit together perfectly.

At first the suspect claimed he wasn't guilty, and that he had broken the ax handle while using it behind his house. But when he came face to face with the police evidence, he changed his plea to guilty.

PILING UP EVIDENCE

A single piece of matching evidence may not be enough to link a suspect to a crime. One match might be coincidence — say, footprints just like the suspect's near a store that was robbed. But what if evidence starts to pile up? As police make more and more matches, the evidence becomes more than coincidental. It becomes conclusive, and adds up to "case closed."

Mystery Toolmarks

hen a harder object hits a softer one it leaves a mark or impression. Police call these dents and scrapes "toolmarks," even if they aren't made by tools. Toolmarks found at the scene of the crime can be important clues to what happened and who was there.

In the Groove

Some toolmarks are made by tools. Thieves forced open a filing cabinet, leaving a scrape. The police suspect the mark was made by a screwdriver blade. They make a test mark on soft metal with the screwdriver they think was used. Every screwdriver makes a different toolmark, since dents and nicks in the tool make distinctive ridges and grooves. If police find a match, they have their tool!

Under a comparison microscope, the tiny grooves and scratches of the test mark (on the left) match the tool-mark made on the filing cabinet (on the right).

Bullet Proof

Bullets have toolmarks on them, too. The inside of a gun barrel has spiral grooves to make the bullet spin — a spinning bullet is more accurate than one that doesn't spin. Every gun makes its own pattern of lines, and it makes the same pattern on every bullet fired from it. Fired bullets have patterns of lines that can be traced to the guns that fired them.

The forensic study of bullets is called ballistics. In the ballistics lab, you'll see specialists shooting into large tubs of water. It's a safe way to fire bullets so that the lines can be compared to the toolmarks on a bullet found at a crime scene. Matching lines are proof that the police have the right gun. Bang!

Two bullets fired by the same gun as shown under a comparison microscope. You can see that the patterns of lines are identical.

Crime Bites

Police were checking a holdup note for fingerprints when they found a bite mark. The thief must have had his hands full with the gun and the bag for the money, so he held the note in his mouth. Once the paper was treated with chemicals, it showed the marks of upper front teeth on the top surface, and a bottom lip mark on the underside. The tooth marks and lip prints were used to identify the thief and put the bite on his crimes!

CLUE IN

A bite mark is a kind of toolmark. Everybody's teeth are different, and make different bite marks. If a criminal leaves a bite mark on something, that's a great clue!

Here's your chance to take a bite at crime solving. There has been a hold-up at an all-night convenience store. Police have one important piece of evidence — a styrofoam cup. The robber had been drinking coffee out of the cup before the hold-up. He left the marks of his bottom teeth on the outside rim of the cup (see right).

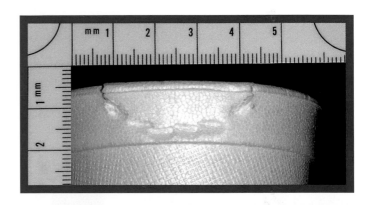

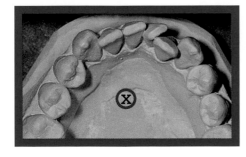

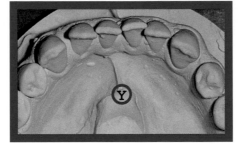

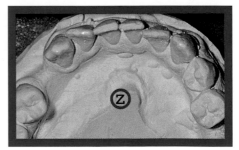

Police searched the neighborhood for people who matched the description given by the counter person at the store. They picked up three possible suspects — let's call them X, Y and Z. Did one of these suspects make the bite mark on the cup? Your job is to find out.

Dental impressions of the three suspects were taken by having them bite into rubbery material, leaving clear bite-mark patterns. From these impressions, a forensic dentist made a mold of each suspect's bottom teeth (see above). Now you have to compare the biting edges of each of these models to the bite mark on the cup.

You'll need a piece of clear plastic — very thin tracing paper or plastic food wrap will do and a pen. Put the plastic over each of the three photos above, and carefully trace the biting edges of the teeth. Label them X, Y and Z to match the labels above.

Now rotate the clear plastic, so that the top of the curve is at the bottom, and the tracing makes a U-shape like the marks on the cup. Place each tracing in turn over the bite mark. Can you find a match? Which suspect left the bite mark on the cup? Should the police arrest X, Y or Z? (Answer on page 61.)

Classy Match

hat do you mean, you found my footprint at the scene of the crime?" says the suspect. "There are hundreds of people walking around with shoes like mine!" But what the suspect doesn't know is that not all of those shoes leave the same footprint.

If the Shoe Fits ...

Matching is done on two levels. First, police see if a piece of evidence and its possible source belong to the same class or kind.

This heel print was found on a piece of glass at a crime scene. The first step is to find out if the suspect has the same size and brand of running shoe.

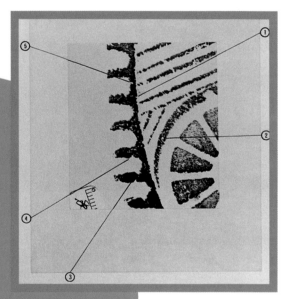

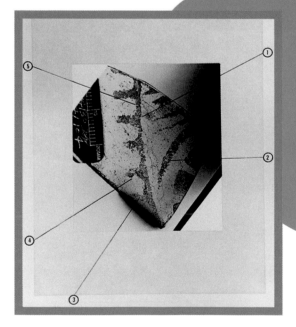

This is the suspect's shoe print. The numbers indicate accidental characteristics that match those on the print found at the crime scene. Note the nicks and worn-down spots.

If they do, police move on to the next level — matching accidental characteristics. Accidental characteristics are marks that make something unique. For example, the shape of a person's foot and the way a person walks change the shape of their shoe. Their shoes will wear down in different spots than on anybody else's shoe. If the accidental characteristics match, police have solid evidence to link the suspect to the crime.

Sweaty Feet?

Scientists can analyze the sweaty impression made by a foot inside a shoe, and match it with the actual foot that wore that shoe. Where was that technology when Cinderella's Prince Charming needed it?

Wired for Sound

Police scientists will go to great lengths just to find the perfect match. In one case, police had a suspect for a murder. They also had the murder weapon — a piece of copper wire with a clear plastic coating. The stereo in the suspect's car used wire that looked identical, and a piece of that was missing. Could police prove that the wire found at the crime scene came from the suspect's car stereo?

It was hard to see if there were marks on the clear plastic, so a police scientist made casts of the plastic coatings. On the casts he could see marks made by the machine that manufactured the wires, and the marks were the same on both wires. Since every machine would make slightly different marks, the wires were both produced by the same machine. But many miles of wire came from that machine. The matching marks on the plastic weren't proof that the wire found at the crime scene came from that particular car stereo, or from a car stereo at all.

So the scientist looked at the copper strands that ran inside the plastic coating. Through a scanning electron microscope, he saw tiny marks on the strands that were identical in both pieces of wire. The scientist found that the wire was manufactured by a company in Fort Worth, Texas. He went to Fort Worth to examine the machine that produced the copper strands, and found a crucial clue. As the machine made the wire, the marks it left on the wire's surface changed. Two sections of the same wire only a metre apart would have different marks on them. If the two pieces of wire had identical marks, then those pieces must have been side-by-side along the wire.

The marks matched! The piece of wire used to commit the crime came from the suspect's stereo. Connecting the suspect to the murder weapon made the case. When the evidence was shown to the court, the murderer was convicted.

The Right Stuff

Two things might look like they match, but it's hard to tell for sure. Are things the same color and texture really made up of the same stuff? Is the chip of glass on the sole of Mr. Suspect's shoe from the window broken during the kidnapping? Is the flake of metal on Ms. Suspect's clothes from the safe drilled open during the robbery? Call in the forensic chemists!

High-Tech Matching

What do you think a microspectrophotometer is? It's a machine that can tell if two bits of fabric were colored by the same batch of dye, and it's just one of the high-tech machines that help police match-make. Scanning electron microscopes magnify objects thousands of times, and also create 3-D images of them for police to compare. Chromagraphs break down substances into tiny molecular parts, so spectrometers can identify them. When lasers and ultraviolet lights are shone on fibers and inks, some glow and some don't. You need more than a magnifying glass to be a good detective these days. Sorry, Sherlock.

Chemistry Class

Forensic chemists get right into the evidence, sometimes on the molecular level! They are experts in finding out what things are made of. They can tell if two samples are made of exactly the same stuff, and if they came from the same source.

Take the case of this hit-and-run accident. A careful search for clues turned up a tiny paint chip stuck to the victim's blue jeans. Could police trace it to the vehicle? The police were in luck — the paint chip was made up of many distinctive layers of paint. Police found a car that had what looked like the same layers of paint on it. But were they really the same?

Forensic chemists used an infrared spectrometer to analyze the layers of paint in the chip. Bingo! Each layer of the chip was identical to each layer of paint on the car. Once police had the right car, identifying the hit-and-run driver was easy.

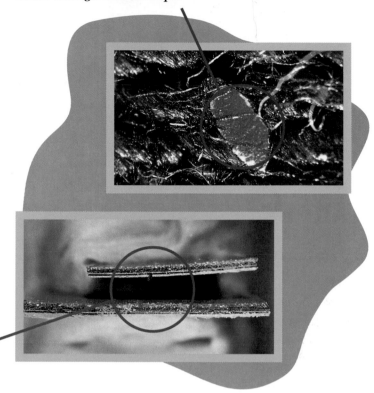

The paint chip found on the victim's jeans was so small that this photo of it was taken through a microscope.

Side views of the paint chip and a paint sample taken from the car show the layers that were analyzed one by one.

CLUE IN

If two things are made of exactly the same chemicals, police can connect them. For example, if the gasoline from a can in the back of a suspect's truck is an exact chemical match with the gasoline used to start a fire, the police may have their arsonist. Chromatography is a colorful way to identify chemicals in a substance. Each chemical shows up as a colored spot on a test strip.

Try this simple chromatography test to match inks that are chemically the same. Black ink contains colors that travel at different speeds along a piece of paper. Different rainbow effects (different chromagraphic results) come from different inks.

1 Find several washable black felt pens to compare.

2 Cut a strip of coffee filter or paper towel for each pen.

3 Put a black dot at the bottom of each strip and record which pen you used to make the dot.

4 One at a time, dip the strips into water. Dip to just below the dot. Make sure the dot stays above water. Hold the strip and allow the water to soak up the strip. Watch what happens to the ink.

5 When you have made all your test strips, challenge someone to use one of the pens (don't look!) to make a dot near the bottom of a new strip. Now test that strip to identify which "mystery" pen was used. Did you pass with flying colors?

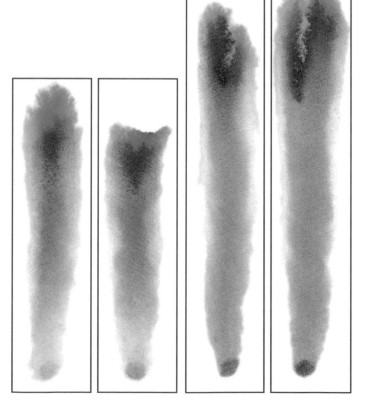

High-Fiber Detection

Some fibers are very small — like the specks of fluff you see floating in the air when the sun shines in a room. It's easy for criminals to miss such tiny evidence they've left behind or are carrying on their clothing. To collect fibers, police use a piece of clear tape, sticky side down. They use laser or ultraviolet light to detect fibers that are almost invisible in normal light.

Fee-Fi(ber)-Fo-Fum

You might think if you've seen one fiber, you've seen them all. But there are so many kinds that fiber detection can yield a lot of clues. Hair and fur are fibers. There are fibers of natural materials like cotton, wool or silk. Synthetic fibers include nylon, polyester, acetate and acrylic, and some glow under special lights. Chemists test fibers to find out if two samples are made of exactly the same chemicals.

Some fibers — white cotton or blue denim — are very common. Other fibers, such as the ones that come from certain carpets, are quite distinctive and uncommon. If police find an unusual carpet fiber on a murder victim, and a carpet made of the same fibers in a suspect's apartment, that's a clue!

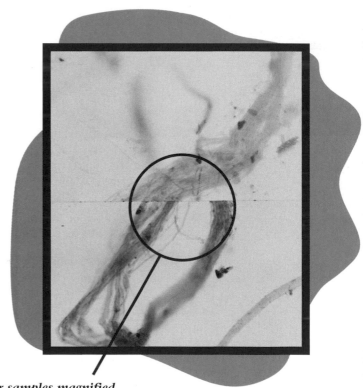

This photo shows two fiber samples magnified 100 times under a comparison microscope. Each sample contains two kinds of fibers — gold strands and tiny flecks of blue. The sample below the horizontal line was taken from the sweater a murder victim was wearing. The sample above the line was found on a suspect's clothing. It's an exact match!

COUNTER-FEITS and FORGERIES

A $1,000 bill is worth a lot. So are checks, passports and birth certificates. Criminals have tried for years to cash in by faking these documents. And now photocopiers, computer scanners and color printers let them make a fake at the push of a button.

Funny Money

 o foil counterfeiters, many countries design paper money that is almost impossible to fake. From special paper to what look like shiny stickers, anti-counterfeiting features take ingenuity to come up with. But they help investigators spot the fakes!

You Know It's the Real Thing...

• **Intaglio printing:** This method uses a printing plate that pushes into the paper with tremendous force. The print seems to be engraved.

• **Fluorescence:** Some bills contain invisible features that glow under ultra-violet light.

• **Security thread:** These strips of polyester are visible inside the paper if you hold the bill in front of a bright light. The security thread shown on this 300 Buckaroo bill has words printed on it, and some glow red under ultraviolet light.

• **Watermarks:** A watermark is a design made by variations in the thickness of the paper. Watermarks are visible when the bill is held up to the light.

• **Color-shifting ink:** Some inks change color when viewed from different angles. Color copiers only pick up one of the colors. Here the rectangle bearing the "300" looks yellow but changes to gold when you tilt it.

• **Microprinting:** Most copiers and scanners can't reproduce tiny lettering. It comes out looking smeared. So most bills include lettering that is so tiny it can be read only with a magnifying glass.

• **Fine line printing:** Some patterns of fine lines are so detailed that copiers and scanners can't print them properly. They come out looking distorted, like ripples in a pond.

color-shifting ink

microprinting

• **Holograms:** Holographic images shift and change color as the bills are tilted back and forth.

• **Spiderlegs:** Silk threads are embedded in the paper. They look like tiny squiggly lines.

CLUE IN

Take a close look at any paper bill and try to spot which anti-counterfeiting features it contains. The higher the denomination of the bill, the more you are likely to find. Hold the bill up to the light to see a watermark, security threads or spider legs. Use a magnifying glass to find microprinting and intaglio printing. Look for a small area printed with color-shifting ink.

Change for a Dollar

A counterfeiter's trick is to change bills to show a higher amount, such as changing $1 to $100. They bleach out the numbers on the bills and reprint them. Or they paste on new corners that say "100" instead of "1." To avoid this, most paper money now has the amount that the bill is worth (for example, "ONE" for a one-dollar bill) microprinted in various places on the bill or printed on the security thread.

spiderlegs

security thread

Photocopy Fakes

Copy machines can be designed to recognize paper money from several countries. If a counterfeiter tries to use the copier to copy money, the copier will print a blank sheet of paper instead.

A copy machine can also print its serial number on every copy it produces. The number is printed in a code, a pattern of almost invisible tiny dots that can appear anywhere on the page. The code can be decoded only with special equipment. This allows police to trace counterfeit money to the copier on which it was made.

19

Bad Checks

S ome counterfeiters fake money, some fake checks. Spotting a fake check is harder than finding a counterfeit bill. And checks are only one kind of valuable papers that are faked. Crooks try to copy and change passports, drivers' licenses, lottery tickets — even store coupons that give a discount off something you buy.

"Check" It Out

In one case, a ring of counterfeiters cashed a fake check worth three-quarters of a million dollars from one of the biggest banks in the United States. They stole a real check, scanned an image of it into their computer, then used the computer to change the amount and the name of the person able to cash the check. Using just the right paper and ink, they printed a check that looked real enough to fool the bank.

To foil counterfeiters, other documents include features found in paper money. The paper used for checks contains watermarks, and some checks are printed with fluorescent ink that appears only under ultraviolet light. Some checks have a special chemical coating that reacts to substances used to erase ink. Some even show the word "Void" in three languages when someone tries to erase the name or the dollar amount. Store coupons sometimes use variable dot patterns that spell out the word "Void" when someone tries to copy them.

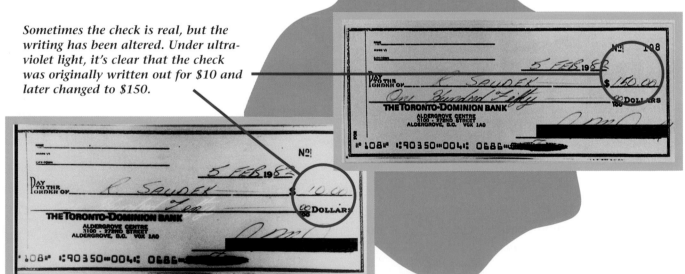

Ink can be erased with bleach or with acetone, which is found in nail-polish remover. This check shows how the chemical coating changes color when bleach (yellow stain on left) and acetone (blue stain on right) are applied.

Sometimes the check is real, but the writing has been altered. Under ultra-violet light, it's clear that the check was originally written out for $10 and later changed to $150.

Altered States

Everyone would like to win the big lottery. So it should come as no surprise that someone would try to cheat their way to the jackpot. In a recent case, two winning lottery tickets were turned in that showed identical numbers — or did they? When police looked at one of the tickets under a microscope, they were able to see that several numbers on that ticket had been erased and rewritten, or altered. The ticket to the right shows the spots where the numbers have been changed and magnifies them. Looking very closely, can you see that the second 1 and the first 9 have suspicious shadows and marks around them? To collect the winnings, you had to be the owner of the ticket shown below!

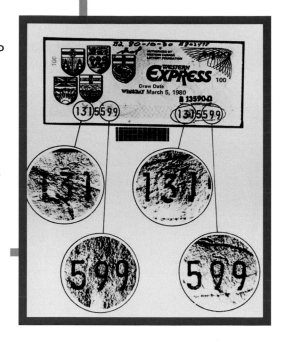

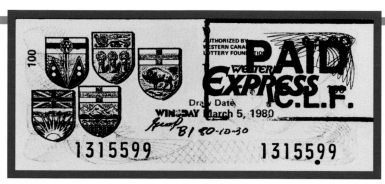

On-the-Job Training

In five years of being a crook, Frank Abagnale cashed in two and a half million dollars' worth of bad checks. He used the fake checks throughout Europe and in every state of the United States. After serving years in prisons in France, Sweden and the U.S., Abagnale decided to switch sides. Now he's a counterfeit expert — he helps banks and companies foil other counterfeiting crooks.

Wrong from write

When you hear "forgery" what do you think of? An expensive painting that's copied and sold as the original? Trying to write like your best friend to send a note as a practical joke? Copying someone's signature on a check for a million dollars? You're right every time. Forgery is making something you put on paper look like it was done by someone else.

Tracing a Forgery

It has happened more than once. Someone steals a checkbook, and practices forging the owner's signature on the first check in the book. Then the forger tries to use the second check to pay for something. But pressing hard on the first check leaves indentations on the checks beneath. Eagle-eyed cashiers notice evidence of practice sessions on the second check where the pen pressed down on the paper.

The DNA Pen

As long as a handwritten document is worth something, it's worth forging. The signature of a really famous person, like a star athlete, is worth a lot of money. So criminals forge signatures of famous people and sell them. Some famous people now use a DNA pen. The owner's saliva is combined with the ink in the DNA pen. Saliva contains molecules of DNA, which are different for every person. That means that every signature that is written with a DNA pen is marked with the owner's unique DNA. If police test a signature and the DNA isn't right, they know it's a fake. (See the chapter "Identifying the Criminal" for more about DNA.)

Police experts compared the handwriting samples to the left of the line with the samples on the right, and concluded that they were made by the same person.

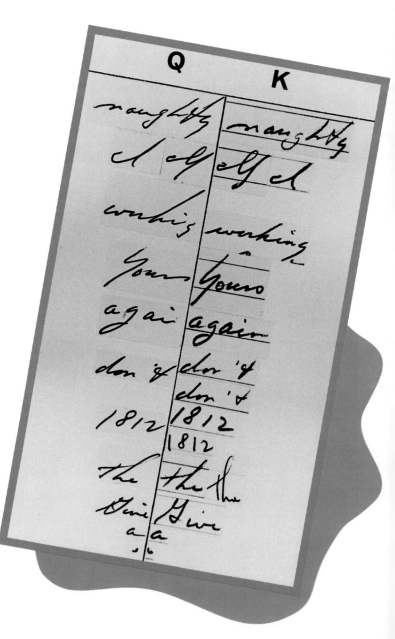

Art Fakes

Since works of art by famous painters can be worth thousands or even millions of dollars, art forgers copy paintings and try to sell the fakes as the originals. Some are caught when experts check the paint and find it contains chemicals that weren't used when the painting is supposed to have been made. Many old paintings are covered with a layer of varnish that develops tiny cracks over time. The cracks are hard to fake, so an expert with a microscope is called in to foil the forger.

CLUE IN

Here are three writing samples. Two are written by the same person, and one is a forgery. Can you spot the forgery? (Answer on page 61.)

B *Please excuse Kathrine from gym.*

A *Please excuse Kathrine from gym.*

C *Please excuse Kathrine from gym*

Hitler's Diary

In April 1983, newspapers and magazines all over the world published what they thought were the diaries of Adolf Hitler. According to the story, the diaries had been rescued from a burning aircraft around the end of World War II (1945), and were found later by a German journalist. The diaries were bought by his magazine for about $13 million.

Why would someone's diaries be worth so much? Hitler was the leader of the Nazi party in Germany before and during World War II. Not only did he lead Germany into the war, but he was responsible for ordering the imprisonment, torture and murder of millions of innocent people. The possibility of new information about the most notorious figure of the 20th century electrified the world.

There was only one problem — the diaries were fake. It took the experts shown below 48 hours to discover that Hitler's signature in the diary didn't match his real one. Even more evidence of the forgery: the paper, ink, glue and binding were all dated as being made after the war. It took only two days to discover the fakes, but it took two years of investigation before the man who forged the diaries was caught. The forger and the journalist were each sentenced to more than four years in prison.

ComPuT-ers and CrimE

It's late at night. Most people are asleep. In front of a glowing computer screen, a hacker is committing a crime. From the privacy of her home she is roaming through cyberspace, breaking into computer systems all over the world. Computers have created a whole new field of crime. But they also help police to solve crimes. Either way, computers deserve investigation . . .

Computer City

Thieves creep through city streets at night and break into buildings to steal any valuable stuff they find inside. Computer thieves break into unlocked or unsecured computer systems to steal valuable information. Computer city is full of crime — so watch out!

Security Clearance Denied...

Not everyone has a computer at home. But almost all workplaces would have to shut down without them. Computers are used to store information, do calculations, print reports, create graphics and much, much more.

Often a company will have many computers linked into a network or system. Each worker, called a user, has a password. Passwords let users log in — connect the computers on their desks to the network — so information can travel between individual computers.

You can think of a company's computer system as being like its building, with offices connected by hallways, and one big front door. Some computer networks have "open doors" — you don't need a password to log in to a public library's computer listings to check what books are there.

Other computer networks containing top-secret military or business information use high-tech security devices to keep out unauthorized users. Before a user can log in, identification — a password, thumbprint or even voiceprint (a "picture" of a spoken word) — must be entered. Another way computer systems keep out interlopers is by scrambling information in the files. Authorized users can decode the info, but for anyone else it's "mission impossible."

Net Crimes

The Internet is like an electronic highway running between computer systems. In just seconds, information travels around the globe through phone lines, cables and wireless networks.

Throughout the world, a billion people are linked to the Internet. They have access to unlimited information — anyone can put anything on the Internet. There are no rules. So some troublemakers use the Internet to spread lies or hate, to publish secrets or to break the law. Tracking down Internet criminals is a new challenge for cybercops.

CLUE IN

To foil hackers, or computer criminals, computer users use secret passwords to access their computer accounts. How could a hacker possibly guess a password from all the words that can be used? Hackers have developed computer programs that try, one by one, every word in a dictionary until they find the one that works!

Which of the following passwords wouldn't be found by a hacker using a program that tries every word in a very thorough dictionary? (Answer on page 61.)

zemindar	exegesis
baifudir	crutnopa
varactor	xanthoma
prolteif	geroleis

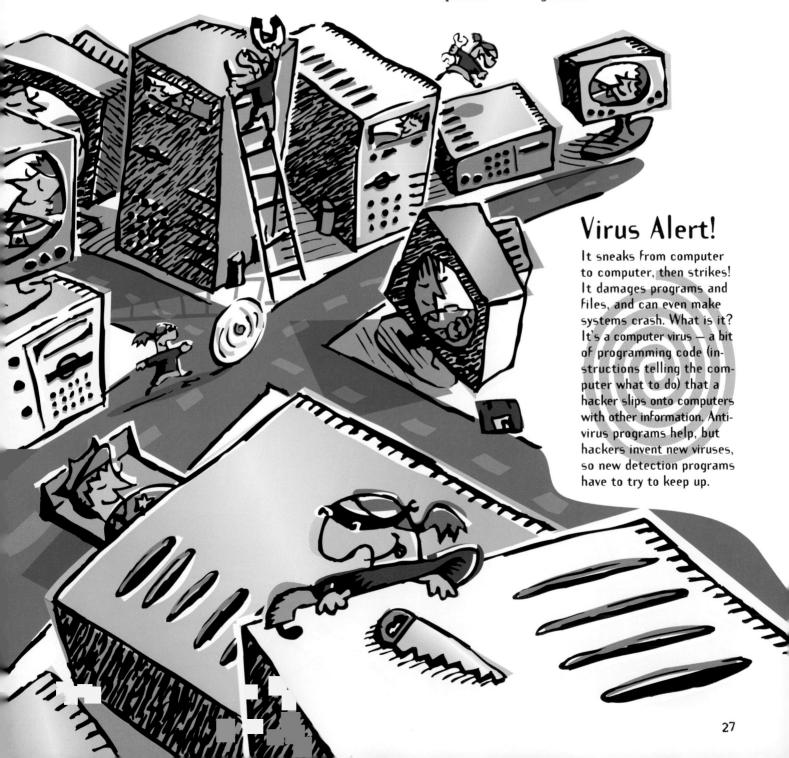

Virus Alert!

It sneaks from computer to computer, then strikes! It damages programs and files, and can even make systems crash. What is it? It's a computer virus — a bit of programming code (instructions telling the computer what to do) that a hacker slips onto computers with other information. Anti-virus programs help, but hackers invent new viruses, so new detection programs have to try to keep up.

CyberCrooks

ackers are computer criminals. With nothing more than a computer and an Internet connection, a hacker can case out a computer system next door or far away. As experts in getting into other people's computers — guessing passwords, finding secret or valuable files — hackers use their skills for mischief or crime.

Break and Enter

Imagine a vandal roaming around your neighborhood, finding doors that haven't been locked, sneaking through holes in gates and getting into all sorts of private places. Hackers are like that. Inside a computer, they can damage important information stored there, steal secrets or make the whole computer system crash. Information they steal can be worth a lot: computers keep records of people's credit cards and bank accounts.

To keep out unwanted intruders, computer users install "firewalls." Hackers who attempt to get through these firewalls to get access to the computers will leave behind "electronic fingerprints." Investigators use these electronic clues to track down the hacker's location.

Hacker Tracking

Hackers are usually caught by tracing their "footsteps" back from the scene of the crime:

• Tsutomu Shimomura found hundreds of files and software programs were stolen from his computer.

• It took him a month to find where the hacker had stashed the stolen data. Friends on the Internet alerted him to a server storing hundreds of millions of bytes of information — his stolen files.

• A trace put on the account led back to the hacker's service provider in San Jose, California. There the trail split — data was coming from modems in Denver, Colorado; Minneapolis, Minnesota; and Raleigh, North Carolina. Government investigators helped pin down Raleigh as the site of the telephone switching system the hacker was using. It looked like the work of Kevin Mitnick.

• Shimomura and a cellular-phone technician drove through Raleigh with a frequency-detecting antenna linked to a laptop computer. It finally homed in on a signal — from Kevin Mitnick's apartment. Before he was tracked down by the cyberdetective, Mitnick had stolen $1 million worth of information and 200,000 credit card numbers, all from the safety of his computer.

Tsutomu Shimomura (above), a computer security expert, became a cyberdetective to catch notorious hacker Kevin Mitnick (right).

Not Just a Game

Some hackers hack just to see if they can get away with it, but their victims lose a lot of money and valuable secrecy. Suppose hackers broke into the systems of a company that develops computer games, and stole the source code for its most popular games. The company could lose thousands and thousands of dollars in sales. And their secret techniques might be sold to competitors, who could copy bits of code into their own software.

The 75-Cent Clue

Clifford Stoll ran a computer system in Berkeley, California. As "superuser" or system administrator, he kept a close eye on the records. One day, Stoll found something weird in the payment record. There was a 75¢ error. One of the thousands of users had used the system for 75¢ worth of time and not been billed for it.

It might sound like a tiny bit of money to worry about. But that 75¢ was the first clue Stoll had to a much bigger problem — that a hacker had broken into Stoll's computer system. Who was it? Stoll spent the next year trying to find out. During that time, he helplessly watched from his computer as the hacker used the system in Berkeley as a starting point to break into military computer systems all across the United States.

Stoll had to be sharp and sneaky himself to shadow the hacker, to keep track of the hacker's activities on the computer without the hacker knowing someone was watching. Stoll even made up huge files full of fake info so the hacker would have lots to read — and would stay connected to his system long enough for the phone company to trace the lines. After a year, the hacker was traced back to his computer – in Germany. An arrest was made by the German police. From a 75¢ clue to the capture of an international hacker. . . now that's cybersleuthing!

For the Record

Investigation takes a lot of brainwork, and a lot of gruntwork — sorting through piles and piles of information to find the one bit that's needed. Good thing there are computers on the side of the law! They might not have the intuition humans have for the brainwork, but they can be programmed to store and sort through lots of information in a very short time.

Computer Print-out

You're an investigator who has found a perfect, complete fingerprint at a crime scene. The thought of comparing that single fingerprint to the millions of fingerprints on file is making you dizzy! It could take months of detailed searching, and guaranteed eyestrain. The good news is that now all fingerprint information is stored in a computer database. A computer can check through 1,200 prints in one second. A human fingerprint expert is needed only at the very end to confirm the computer's match.

There are other computer databases that speed an investigation along. There's one that records ballistic fingerprints — the identifying marks left on each bullet fired by a particular gun. In minutes, the computer can match the pattern of grooves left on one bullet with bullets recovered from other crime scenes. With luck, the ballistic information can lead the police to a suspect, like a shot! Soon police computer records may include ballistic fingerprints for every gun registered.

Paint by Numbers

Remember the hit-and-run case (page 15) where the only clue was a chip of paint from a car? Police can chemically analyze layers of primer and paint in even the smallest paint chip. When the results are entered in an automotive paint computer database, the computer can identify the make, model and year of cars painted with those layers.

The next step is to find the particular car, using a computer database that lists the registered owners of automobiles. If the car in a hit-and-run is an unusual make and model, there might only be a few matching cars near the crime scene. Another database contains the addresses of those licensed owners, who might each get a little visit from investigators with questions about their whereabouts at the time the crime was taking place. . . .

Data-Basic

Stacks and stacks of police records provide information for databases of all kinds — criminal records, DNA samples, missing children, registered firearms, pictures and descriptions of banned weapons and much, much more.

If It Weren't for Bad Luck . . .

In Baton Rouge, Louisiana, 15-year-old Jimmy Laroux was having a bad day that just kept getting worse. At school, his record-breaking kick of a soccer ball broke a window. On his way home, he tore his new jeans climbing over a fence. Then, walking by an apartment building, he was stopped by the police for questioning. Just ten minutes earlier, a thief had broken into the building through a window and stolen some cash. And along comes Jimmy, with a brand-new tear in his jeans and pieces of broken glass stuck in the soles of his running shoes!

The police analyzed the glass from the broken window in the apartment building. They entered the information into a database and found that the glass was very common. Even if the glass on Jimmy's shoes was identical, it wouldn't prove anything. And it turned out that the glass on Jimmy's shoes (from the school window) was manufactured 30 years earlier. There was no way it could have come from the newer apartment window.

Jimmy was free to go. The police concentrated on other evidence to catch the thief, and Jimmy started earning money to pay for the broken window.

CyberCops

atabases hold lots of clues to a successful investigation. But police find all kinds of ways for computers to help them solve crimes and catch crooks. From putting together a profile of a criminal to reconstructing the scene of a crime, computers rule in crime investigation.

Crime Spree

What are serial crimes? That's when several similar crimes are committed by one person over a period of time. It's hard to know if one criminal is responsible for more than one, say, murder or arson.

Police working on a case might not realize that a crime with the same "modus operandi" (the details of how the crime was committed) had occurred somewhere else. Similarities in the M.O. would make them look for the work of a serial criminal. If information about every crime is put into a computer, police have a way of looking for crimes that follow a pattern.

Drag-Net

Criminals often commit their crimes in neighborhoods that they know well and where they feel comfortable, usually near where they live or work. A computer program helps police mark out this "comfort zone" and locate a serial criminal. Police plot the location of serial crimes on a computer map. Thousands of calculations later, the computer predicts the most probable neighborhood for the suspect's home. As police focus their search on suspects who live in that neighborhood, their net draws tighter and tighter. . . .

On this computer-generated map of a criminal's "comfort zone," the warmer colors mark "hot spots" in the city where the crimes are concentrated.

Going Global

Faster than a speeding bullet, computers can send information almost instantly around the world. It doesn't matter whether the receiving computer is in the next room, in a patrol car across the city or in another police detachment across the country. Police can compare notes on crimes that took place in different cities yet seem quite similar—and might be the work of the same criminal.

Plans are forming to link the computer systems of police forces around the world. Soon there may be nowhere a criminal can go to escape from his crimes.

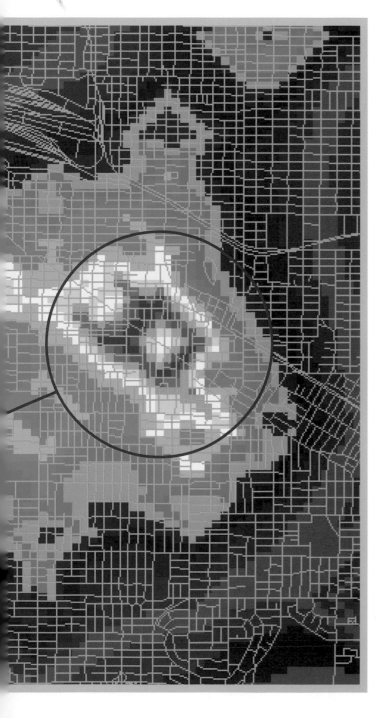

Instant Replay

At the crime scene, investigators try to piece together what really happened. If it was an automobile accident, they'll be measuring skid marks to calculate the driver's speed and direction. If there was shooting, they might be examining bullet holes in the walls and working out where the shots were fired from. They can tell a lot from spatters of blood on a wall. The size, shape and pattern of the drops help them calculate the trajectory (path) of the blood, the force of the blow, and whether the attacker was right- or left-handed.

Computer programs take measurements from photos of the scene, and do mathematical calculations to re-create details of the crime. Animation and 3-D graphics programs let police replay a crime in various ways and from different angles. For instance, they can see how much a driver might have been able to view on a foggy night.

Profile of an Arsonist

Someone might set fire to a building for the insurance money, or to hurt one particular victim. But sometimes arson is a serial crime. And where a pattern exists, computers can help spot it. In a case in Canada, an arsonist had been torching garages for eight months, seemingly at random. It wasn't that the police had no leads to follow – they had received hundreds of tips about the crime. They just didn't know where to begin.

First police created a geographic profile of the arsonist. They plotted the location of all his fires on a computer map. The computer pinpointed by postal code the neighborhood where the suspect most likely lived.

One tip many people had given the police was that a dark blue van was seen in the areas around the time of the fires. Going to the computer database of vehicle registrations, police pulled out the names and addresses of all owners of dark blue vans living in that neighborhood. By comparing the postal codes with the addresses of the blue van owners, the police came up with a shortlist of suspects.

One of the van owners seemed uncomfortable when police questioned him. Inside his van, police found gasoline and rags. Further analysis linked this evidence with the arsons. The suspect was arrested.

Authorized Personnel Only!

"Photo identification card, please. What's your password?"

Only authorized people can access private bank accounts, log onto company computers or enter nuclear power facilities. They use secret passwords, photo identification or plastic identity cards that allow them to pass through the security gate. Trouble is, passwords can be forgotten or overheard. Identity cards can be stolen or faked.

One thing that can't be easily stolen or faked is you! There's nobody else exactly the same as you. Today, using biometric technologies, a computer can scan you and transform you into a set of measurements, creating a unique "mathematical description" that can be stored in the computer. So if someone comes along pretending to be you, even if they look a lot like you and are carrying your identification, the computer will know better.

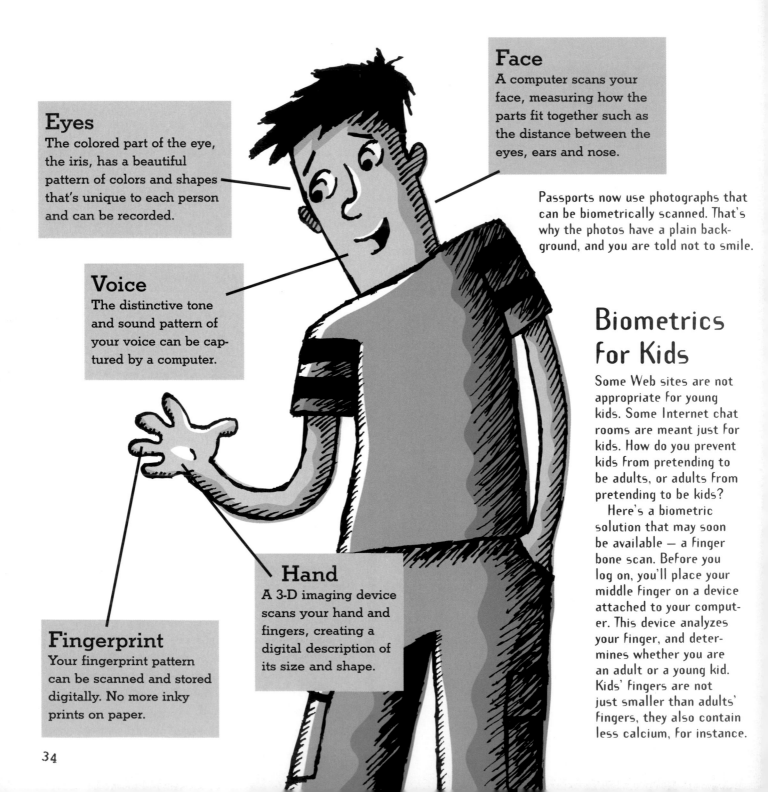

Eyes
The colored part of the eye, the iris, has a beautiful pattern of colors and shapes that's unique to each person and can be recorded.

Voice
The distinctive tone and sound pattern of your voice can be captured by a computer.

Fingerprint
Your fingerprint pattern can be scanned and stored digitally. No more inky prints on paper.

Hand
A 3-D imaging device scans your hand and fingers, creating a digital description of its size and shape.

Face
A computer scans your face, measuring how the parts fit together such as the distance between the eyes, ears and nose.

Passports now use photographs that can be biometrically scanned. That's why the photos have a plain background, and you are told not to smile.

Biometrics for Kids
Some Web sites are not appropriate for young kids. Some Internet chat rooms are meant just for kids. How do you prevent kids from pretending to be adults, or adults from pretending to be kids?

Here's a biometric solution that may soon be available — a finger bone scan. Before you log on, you'll place your middle finger on a device attached to your computer. This device analyzes your finger, and determines whether you are an adult or a young kid. Kids' fingers are not just smaller than adults' fingers, they also contain less calcium, for instance.

34

IdenTi-fying the crimiNal

"**Y**ou figure I did the crime," says the suspect in the interrogation room. "So, prove it!" Police think they know who's guilty, but they have to prove it in court. For years, the only sure proof was an eyewitness. But what about mistaken identity?

The Art of ID

L et's say you actually witnessed a crime. You saw the thief and know what she looks like. Well . . . sort of, anyway. The police will probably call in a forensic artist to work with you to come up with a drawing of the thief. How old was the suspect? What was the hair like? You might look through a "features book" to pick out features that look like the suspect's.

Face to Face with Crime

Computer programs can be used to create faces using a selection of features. But many forensic artists still do most of their work freehand. When a witness says, "That looks a lot like her, but could you make her just a bit meaner?" it is usually easier to do that by hand.

Police will put the sketch in the newspaper or on a poster tacked up around town. They hope that somebody who sees that drawing will recognize the face and tell them who it is.

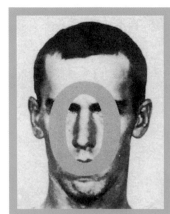

When you look at a sketch drawn by a forensic artist from a witness's description, and compare it with a photo of the actual person, you can see how well a police sketch can work to identify a criminal.

Here are several "noses with narrow bridges" from the FBI features book.

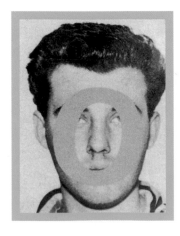
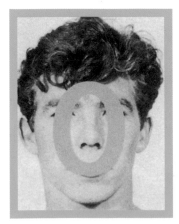
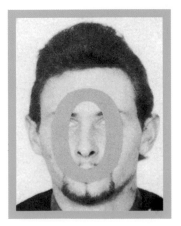

Not Just Another Pretty Face

Maybe you're thinking, "Hey, I can draw better than that!" That's because the forensic artist who drew the picture is not interested in a pretty drawing or a good-looking portrait. What is most useful in investigation is a picture that someone will look at and say, "Yeah, I know who that person is." Most people remember unusual features, so that's what the drawing will emphasize — a big jaw, or a pudgy nose, or teeth that stick out. It's a bit like a caricature. The hardest suspect to draw and recognize would be one of average height, of average build, with average features and no distinguishing marks!

Good with Faces

To be a forensic artist, drawing skills are not enough. A forensic artist also has to be able to work well with witnesses who have just been involved in a crime. They may still feel scared or nervous. If the artist helps them relax and feel comfortable, they will do a better job of answering questions and remembering details.

Growing Older...

A computer-aging program can help police artists make a face look years older. That's how they can come up with current pictures of criminals who have been on the run for a few years, or of kids who have been missing for a long time.

Photo Finish

If you watch movies or police shows on TV, you've seen witnesses look at a line-up to identify a suspect. But it takes time to gather people matching a general description to make the line-up. Sometimes a photo line-up is better.

Harry Dekoff was ready to close his sporting goods store when a man wearing a blue jacket and a Chicago Bulls cap came in. He checked that the store was empty, pulled a gun and demanded all the money in the till. With $6,200, the thief left in a car that was idling on the street. Harry described the thief to the police artist and the sketch was distributed to police detachments. Two weeks later, a guard at the jail noticed that prisoner 123456, just convicted of robbing a convenience store, looked a lot like the sketch.

The investigators put together a photo line-up. They used color mugshots, taken when a criminal is jailed and showing front and side views of the face. When Harry looked at the 12 pictures of six men with similar features, he pointed to the photos of prisoner 123456. The suspect confessed to the robbery of the sporting goods store, and his sentence was extended.

Fingerprints

There's no one just like you, or just like anyone else. Look carefully at your fingers. Notice the pattern of lines on the pads of your fingertips that give your fingers extra grip. They are also a tool for identifying people. Nobody else has a fingerprint exactly the same as yours, not even your identical twin. And fingerprints don't change from birth to death.

Oops! And Oops Again!

It was a case of mistaken identity that happened not once, but twice, in the years before police started using fingerprint identification.

In 1897 an innocent man, Adolph Beck, was arrested for cheating women of their money. Actually another man, William Thomas, was the crook, but Beck looked so much like Thomas that the women swore Beck was the one who had tricked them. After five years in jail Beck was released, but he was almost immediately arrested again for more crimes that Thomas had committed. Fortunately, before Beck could go to jail again, a policeman on the case saw Thomas in another jail (he had been arrested for trying to sell stolen goods). Beck was released.

Would you be able to tell one man from the other? Several eyewitnesses couldn't. But before fingerprinting was used to identify criminals, eyewitness testimony might have often convicted the wrong person.

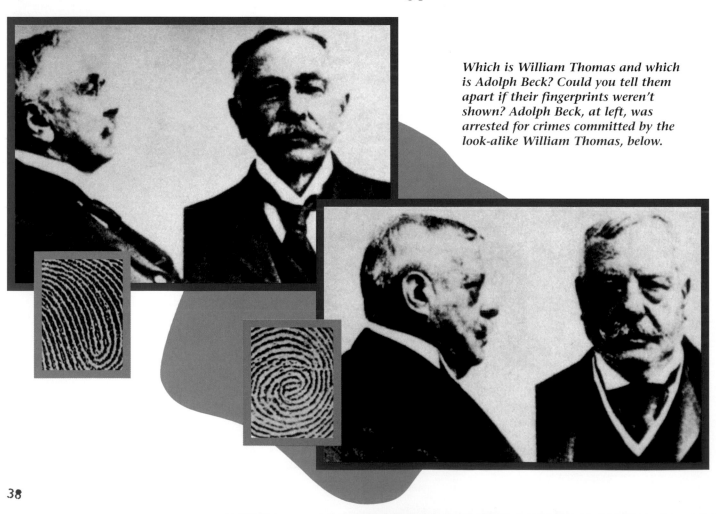

Which is William Thomas and which is Adolph Beck? Could you tell them apart if their fingerprints weren't shown? Adolph Beck, at left, was arrested for crimes committed by the look-alike William Thomas, below.

Print Patterns

All fingerprints can be divided into three pattern classes: loops, whorls and arches.

Loops (60–65% of people have this kind) can start from left or right. Two loops (one right and one left) can curl around each other.

Whorls (30–35%) have a full circle at the center.

Arches (5%) have a clear arch shape around the center, with other lines arching around.

Foiled by Fingerprints

In 1963, thirty men jumped a train traveling from Glasgow, Scotland, to London, England. They made off with mailbags containing more than £2,500,000 (that's worth about U.S.$43 million today). The Great Train Robbery was one of the best-organized robberies ever — almost!

After the robbery, the thieves hid out at a farmhouse where they divided up the money. Someone was supposed to wipe away the fingerprints, but no cleaning up was done. Police found fingerprints all over the place.

Within days, most of the robbers were arrested, although two of the ringleaders were never caught. Most of the money was never found. The thieves who were brought to trial were given long prison sentences, except for one. His fingerprints had been found on a Monopoly game at the farm, but his lawyer argued that since it was an old game, his prints might have been put on to it at some other time in the past. He was set free.

Fingering the Culprit

t the scene of the crime, police investigators search for fingerprints. Fingers get sweaty and oily, so everyone who touches an object leaves behind their very own "stamp" — a pattern of little ridges. Some prints are visible, like a sooty or bloody handprint left on a wall. Most are latent, which means they are invisible to the human eye.

Lifting Prints

Police use fine powders that stick to faint, oily prints and make them more visible. Dark powders show up on light-colored surfaces; white or gray powder is used for dark surfaces. Police can use chemicals that react with oil and make the prints visible. Or they use ultraviolet and laser lights. Under the blue-green light of the laser, prints that were invisible actually glow.

In seconds, police can take a digital photo of a print and send it by photophone to a computerized fingerprint data bank to check for a match.

To see fingerprints on something like a plastic bag, police use a particular kind of glue. In an airtight container with the plastic bag, the glue gives off fumes that cause chemicals to build up on the oily surface of the print. The print is then treated with a special dye to make it visible.

CLUE IN

Become a fingerprint expert. First make a fingerprint, then lift and dust one. It takes practice to get it right.

1 Rub a pencil on a sheet of white paper. Then rub the tip of your index finger on the pencil mark until it is covered with pencil lead.

2 Put the sticky side of a piece of clear tape over the finger, and carefully peel the tape off. Stick the tape to a sheet of yellow or white paper. Wash your finger.

3 Examine your fingerprint (a magnifying glass is helpful) and decide what pattern class it is (see page 39). Do all your fingers have the same print pattern?

Have a member of your family or a friend make a mystery print. It will be more fun if you don't know for sure who made the print. The person making the mystery print should first make their fingertips oily by rubbing them through their hair or handling a few potato chips. Then they should press a finger on a smooth, flat surface (like a shiny tabletop).

1 Choose contrasting powder to dust the print – white talcum powder for a dark surface; black pencil powder (made by rubbing a pencil tip with fine sandpaper) or cocoa powder for a light surface. You won't need much.

2 Brush the powder very lightly over the print using a soft feather or a soft paintbrush. Gently! When the print starts to appear, stroke in the direction of the ridges.

3 When the fingerprint is fully developed, press a piece of clear sticky tape on the print. Press down hard on the tape and rub it well with your fingernail.

4 Peel off the tape carefully and stick it onto a piece of paper that contrasts in color with the powder.

5 Take fingerprints from your family and friends (press their fingers on a washable ink pad and then paper, or use the method at left). Label each one. Now check the mystery print against the prints you have labeled. Can you identify the mystery print?

DNA - It's in the Genes

 hat's DNA? It's the greatest breakthrough in forensic science since the discovery of fingerprints. DNA, short for deoxyribonucleic acid, is found in cells of a living body. Each of your DNA molecules contains genetic information that makes you look like you, and not like a turtle or a cat or your brother. Only identical twins have identical DNA.

You and Only You

Police can get a DNA sample from almost any part of the body, including saliva, blood, urine or hair. Comparing two DNA samples tells the police whether they came from the same person or not.

Say a suspect in a murder investigation claims she's never been near the victim, and provides a DNA sample by scraping a cotton swab along the inside of her cheek. Police compare this sample with DNA taken from a hair found on the victim's clothes. If the samples match, the hair came from the suspect. It's a good bet she's lying.

DNA can link a suspect with a crime, but more important, it can clear an innocent person. In Canada, Guy Paul Morin was set free in 1995, eleven years after he was convicted of murder. While Morin was in jail, the scientific techniques for collecting and testing DNA samples improved. A person's DNA code doesn't change over time, so analysts can get an accurate reading after many years. Upon retesting, Morin's DNA did not match the samples left by the killer at the crime scene. DNA proved that Morin was innocent.

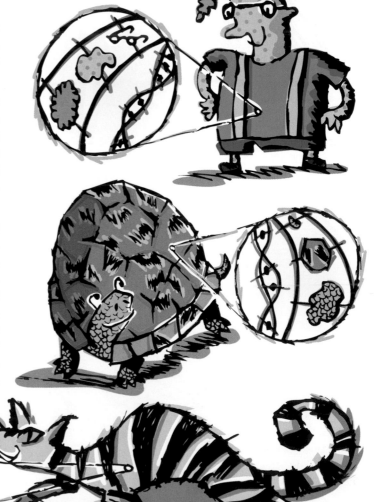

Autorad-ical Proof

DNA Data

A single DNA molecule consists of two spiral strands linked in what is known as a double-helix formation. If you stretched all the DNA from a single cell end to end, it would be more than 2 metres (6 feet) long.

Comparing DNA is a complicated process. Tests are done at different points along a strand or molecule of DNA. The results, one row or *lane* with dark bands for each test, are placed side by side and compared in an autoradiogram (autorad for short).

DNA samples from different people give different patterns. If two lanes show the same pattern, the DNA samples probably come from the same person. To make sure, scientists will compare more fragments of the two DNA molecules to see if they, too, create identical autorad patterns.

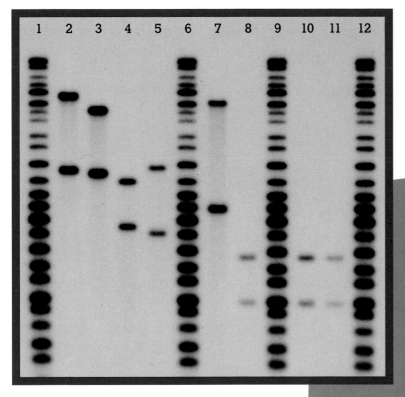

There's a lot of information in the autorad at left, all shown as dark bands arranged in lanes. Lanes 1, 6, 9 and 12 are markers to measure the size of the sample DNA bands. Lanes 2–5 are controls to make sure the results are of good enough quality to show up as bands. Lanes 7 and 8 show two known samples of DNA. The DNA in lanes 10 and 11 match the DNA in lane 8.

CLUE IN

You are investigating a robbery. The victim woke up in the middle of the night to find someone in his apartment. He surprised the thief, and they struggled. Both were bleeding from minor injuries by the time the thief escaped out the window. The victim said it was too dark to tell who the thief was, but that it might have been a plumber who had been working in the building the day before.

You test **DNA** samples from the victim (shown in lane 2) and the suspect (shown in lane 3). You compare them with the **DNA** tests of a blood stain found at the scene of the crime that might contain both the victim's blood and the thief's (shown in lane 5) and with a blood stain found on the suspect's work clothes (shown in lane 6).

The suspect denies that he broke into the apartment, and claims the blood on his clothes was from a nosebleed he had. Take a look at the results to the right. Is he telling the truth? (Answer on page 61.)

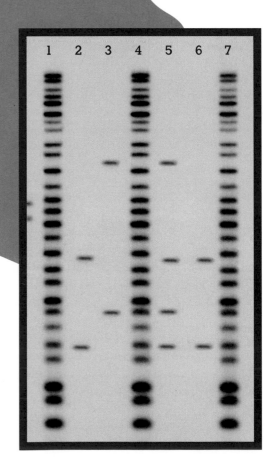

More DNA Evidence

Don't sneeze! You'll leave DNA on this book! It's hard not to leave some of your DNA behind wherever you go. Super sleuths today can even get a DNA sample from a smudged fingerprint. One time, the police solved a burglary using DNA evidence found on the doorknob of the house. It came from invisible skin cells that flaked off the burglar's hand when he turned the knob. In another case, the weapon used in a bank heist was a tree branch wrapped with hockey tape at one end. Police got their DNA sample from skin cells found on the sticky side of the hockey tape.

Generating a "Hit" (Ouch!)

Police have access to two DNA data banks. One contains DNA profiles from criminals convicted of serious crimes. The other contains DNA from crime scenes. Here's how it works. If police are investigating a new crime, they can submit a profile of DNA found at the crime scene. Maybe they'll get a hit — the DNA will match DNA found at a previous crime scene. It looks like the same criminal was involved in both crimes! Or perhaps the DNA will match a previously convicted offender already listed in the data bank, who is now back in the community. Time to pay him or her a visit!

Anytime DNA from a newly convicted criminal is added to the data bank, it may show a match with a "cold case" — a previously unsolved crime. Bingo!

Future Flash

Scientists are working on a way to tell when DNA was left at a crime scene. It has to do with the way the DNA material changes over time. So in future, investigators might be able to prove not just that a suspect was at the crime scene, but when he was there.

Signed, Sealed and Convicted

A Seattle investigator was working on an unsolved, 20-year-old murder case. At the time of the crime, there hadn't been enough proof to convict the prime suspect. But with recent advances in DNA science, lab technicians were able to come up with DNA evidence from the crime scene. Trouble was, investigators didn't have a DNA sample from the suspect to compare it with, and the suspect had moved across the country.

The investigator wrote a letter to the suspect. It invited him to join a class-action lawsuit that would return money to people who had overpaid their parking tickets. The letter said that to participate in this lawsuit and get some of the money, the suspect should fill out a form and mail it back in the envelope provided.

You can guess what happened. Police collected DNA from the saliva used to seal the return envelope, and matched it to DNA from the murder scene. The suspect was convicted and is now sending his mail from a jail cell.

CASE FILE

IdeNti-fying tHe Victim

The trail that leads to the criminal often starts with the victim. A body is found, and police need to know who the person was and what caused the death. It might seem gruesome, but the body may be the only piece of evidence police have. The victim can't speak, so the remains have to give the police clues to find the perpetrator of the crime.

The Bare Bones of the Case

Sometimes all that's left of a body by the time police discover it is a skeleton. Or police may find some bones that have been chewed and scattered by wild animals. Or there will be just a few small, charred bone fragments recovered from a fire pit. What information can you get from bones? A lot, if you are a forensic anthropologist.

Talking Skeletons

Anthropologists study the evolution of human beings — how they have changed over thousands of years. Most of their clues to what human beings were like long ago come from ancient bones that have been discovered. So anthropologists know bones. They recognize small differences in bones, or marks on bones that can provide information about the dead person.

Skull shape can be a clue to the ancestry of the person, and whether the person was male or female: male skulls are usually larger, thicker and heavier than female skulls, and males have a more sloping forehead and a squarer chin. Teeth can provide clues about age and much more (see "Clues from Teeth" on page 48). The shoulder blades would show if the shoulder muscles that attached to it were very large on one side. That would mean the person used that shoulder a lot, say as a baseball pitcher, or a carpenter who banged a lot of nails. Leg bone length can show how tall a person was, since taller people usually have longer legs. Fracture lines show where bones have been broken and healed some time in the past. A broad pelvic bone indicates that the person was a female. The small bones in a person's wrist area give clues to the person's age, since the bones there fuse together as a person gets older.

What can a skeleton tell you about its owner? Here are the sorts of things forensic anthropologists look at:

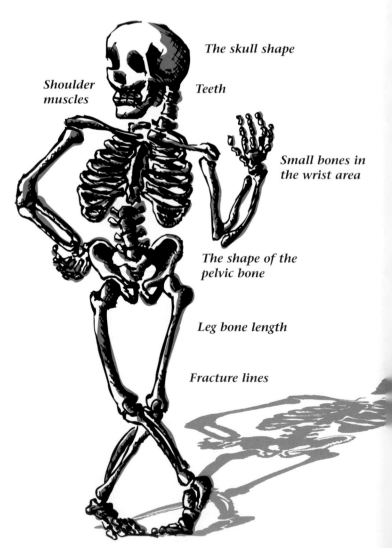

The skull shape

Shoulder muscles

Teeth

Small bones in the wrist area

The shape of the pelvic bone

Leg bone length

Fracture lines

The Missing Link

Near Vancouver, a skull (top right) was found. It was missing the lower jawbone, so dental records couldn't be used to identify it. A forensic anthropologist could tell it belonged to a white male, between 67 and 77 years old.

Checking their missing persons file, the police learned that a 72-year-old white man (bottom right) had disappeared seven years before. He had been living in a house less than ten blocks away from where the skull was found.

When a photo of the missing man was superimposed over a photo of the skull (bottom far right), the two matched up perfectly. Even the man's nose, which twisted slightly to the right, was matched by the skull underneath. The police had finally found their missing person.

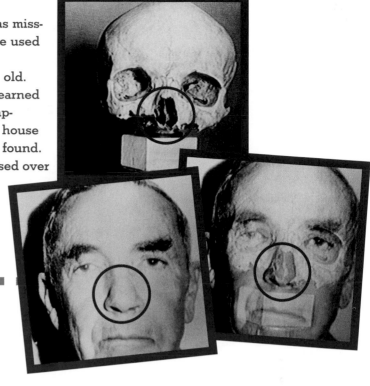

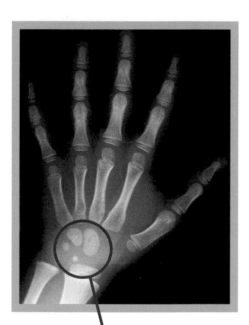

In this x-ray of a child's hand, the bones in the wrist are still separate. In an adult's hand they would be fused together.

The Bear Bones

When police are called in to look at some bones, the first thing they do is determine whether the bones are human. Often they turn out to be bear bones. As you can see from the x-ray photo below, the bones of a bear's paw look amazingly like those of a human hand (except for the claws).

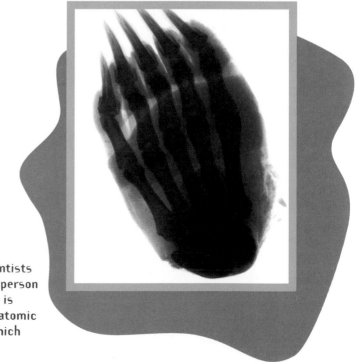

You Are What You Eat!

Bodies, including bones, are made of atoms. Scientists can analyze these atoms to find out what food a person has been eating. A Mexican diet with lots of corn is different from a Japanese diet heavy on fish. So atomic clues can reveal where a victim probably lived, which may help police identify who he or she was.

Investigations with Teeth

Teeth are tough. Even when the rest of a body is unrecognizable or gone, teeth survive. And each person's teeth are different. Biting and chewing changes your teeth. So does the work of a dentist. Your teeth aren't like anyone else's, so teeth can be used to make a positive identification.

Dental ID

When a forensic dentist (or odontologist) is called in to examine teeth, he or she will use some of the same procedures that you might have had in the dentist's chair. Just like a regular dental examination, the dentist starts by making a chart to record the location of cavities, fillings and spaces where teeth are missing. A forensic dentist might take an impression by pressing the teeth into rubber-like material, so the teeth leave a clear pattern. If the police think they know who the teeth belong to, they get dental records from that person's dentist. The forensic dentist compares the charts and x-rays to see whether there is a match.

Clues from Teeth

A forensic dentist can read clues in teeth about the person they belong to. For example, teeth can show the approximate age of the person: young children have baby teeth, with adult teeth hidden in the gums. The older someone is, the more wear on the teeth and the more dental work. Sometimes whether the person was right- or left-handed can be determined by looking at how a toothbrush has worn down the teeth. To tell whether the person was poor or wealthy, a dentist checks how expensive the dental work is. Teeth can even indicate the person's work or hobbies: a groove could be caused when someone holds things in the mouth — like a carpenter holding nails between her teeth. A pipe smoker may have a different-shaped groove on the front teeth. And what about a trumpet player?

CLUE IN

There has been a plane crash, and the wreck of the plane exploded in flames. All four passengers — Mr. Black, Ms. Brown, Ms. Gold and Mr. Green — died. Only their teeth remain to identify them. The families want to be able to bury their loved ones. Police have

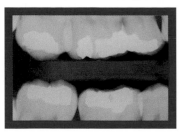

collected the dental records of all four passengers to help you identify which body is which.

The picture on the left shows a postmortem ("after death") x-ray from one of the bodies at the crash. Compare it carefully with the four antemortem ("before death") x-rays police have collected to see if you can find a match. (Answer on page 61.)

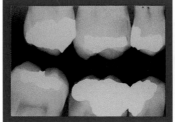
Mr. Black

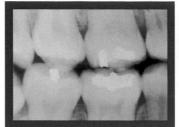
Ms. Gold

Ms. Brown

Mr. Green

Open Wide!

Teeth change over time, which is why they aren't as reliable for indentifying people as fingerprints are. And thanks to fluoride, people get fewer cavities these days — which means fewer dental clues. But now some dentists are attaching a tiny disk to an upper molar of each patient. The pin-head-sized disk contains a 12-number code that identifies the person. If a body with one of these disks is found, police only have to make a quick phone call to the dental registry to identify the person.

Making a Face

Who was this person? Police have found bones and a skull, but the face is unrecognizable. This is a job for a forensic artist. The artist can draw a picture or make a model of what the person probably looked like. Then somebody might be able to put a name to the face.

Building from the Ground Up

How does the artist start? The bones can give some information, like the person's sex. Strands of hair might prove the hair color. The remains of a belt would show what size pants the person was wearing, and give clues to the person's build.

The rest of the clues would come from the skull. The skull shows the shape of the face, and how the eyes, nose and mouth are placed. Forensic artists use a chart to calculate how much tissue (fat, muscle and skin) is likely to be on each part of the skull. Feel your face with your fingertips. How much soft tissue is on your cheeks, your forehead or the tip of your nose? The pictures below show a skull reconstruction in progress.

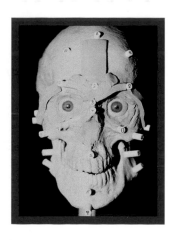 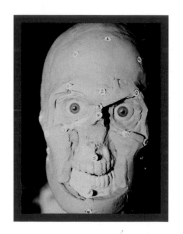  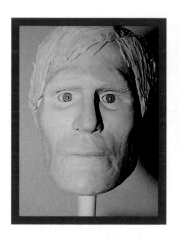

An artist uses modeling clay to build up "tissue" on the skull and re-create the original shape of the head. The white pegs with numbers on them show how deep the tissue should be. The eyes are made of glass.

As a result of this skull reconstruction, the body was identified. The black-and-white photo shows what the person really looked like before his death.

Cooperative Crime Solving

Forensic experts can often help each other out. Construction workers on a site in northern Ontario found a skull missing a lower jaw. Police were able to give the forensic artist some information — that the victim was a woman and her approximate age. But the artist felt that, without the lower jaw, he would be guessing too much.

Call in the forensic dentist. He took information about the shape of the skull, fed it into a computer database and came up with the most likely shape for the lower jaw.

He passed his sketches on to the artist, who was then able to do this sketch.

Hidden DNA

As you learned in the last chapter, DNA can be used to identify criminals. And DNA is used to identify victims too. For instance, if fire or force make the remains of victims unrecognizable, samples of DNA from the bodies could be matched with known samples (such as hair left on a hairbrush). Their remains can be identified.

DNA for the Birds

All living things — including birds — have DNA. Police in Britain used DNA tests to prove that a man was illegally selling wild peregrine falcons. Peregrine falcons (below) are endangered so, to protect their numbers in the wild, only falcons bred in captivity can be legally sold. A dealer claimed that the 20 young birds he had for sale were all the chicks of the three pairs of adult birds he owned. DNA tests proved otherwise. They showed that the birds had come from six sets of parents. The birds must have been captured from the wild. The dealer was sentenced to 18 months in jail.

Dental DNA

DNA can survive for many years, and police scientists need only a tiny amount of DNA material to make an identification. In one case, police were trying to identify a burn victim. A forensic dentist was able to extract a tiny sample of DNA from a nerve inside the victim's tooth. The wisdom tooth was embedded in the gums, which partially protected it from the fire. It was the only usable DNA on the whole body.

All A-Clone

Remember the book and movie *Jurassic Park*? DNA extracted from dinosaur blood inside a mosquito preserved in amber for millions of years was used to make dinosaurs. It was just a story, right? Well, scientists actually do have DNA from specimens in amber — a 30-million-year-old bee and a 120-million-year-old weevil. And in February 1997, a whole sheep was cloned from the DNA of another sheep. The future is bright for DNA evidence. Imagine if police could take a single hair from a crime scene and use the information in it to work up a physical description of the person it came from!

At the Crime Scene

Every crime scene has a story to tell, if you know what to look for. Investigators keep their eyes peeled for evidence about what happened, how it happened, when it happened and where it happened, to help them re-create the crime. They find clues in unlikely places!

If Trees Could Talk...

But trees *can* talk — to a forensic botanist. What could a tree say that would be useful in a police investigation? Because plants are rooted in place, and grow over a certain amount of time, they can help establish when and where a crime took place. And everything a tree tells a forensic botanist might help determine the circumstances of the crime.

Growth Rings

If police find a skeleton in the forest, they will call in a forensic botanist to look for evidence. The botanist's best clue would be a small tree pushed over crooked when the body was placed on the ground. The botanist will cut across the stem and look at the growth rings. Growth rings tell how old a tree is — one circle forms each year. They also tell how a tree grew through each year.

If something leaned against a tree or pushed it over, the growth rings from that year and later would be squished together on one side. It's easy to count back on the rings to see how many years ago the event took place.

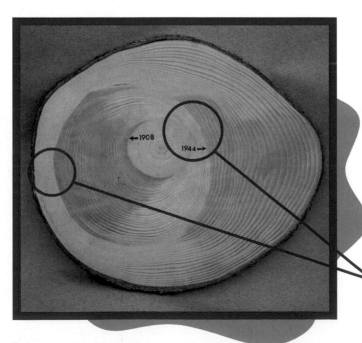

Another growth ring clue: the faster a tree grows, the wider apart the growth rings are. Dead animals and plants add nutrients to the soil as they break down. So a decomposing body can make plants grow more quickly. Again, a quick count back on the rings tells a forensic botanist when it started.

Growth rings show that this tree leaned to the side not once, but twice. The rings at the far left are squished from 1944 onwards. That shows they were on the upper side of the tree, so it must have been leaning to the right. The growth rings in the near left circle show that for the years between 1908 and 1944 the tree leaned to the left.

The Pollen Trace

Pollen grains from plants are microscopic — so tiny they are easily carried to or away from a crime scene. Since different pollens grow in different places, pollen can link people and evidence to a particular spot. If pollen on a body is foreign to the place where it was found, it's a clue that the body has been moved from somewhere else. Police also use pollen found in illegal drug shipments to trace drugs to their country of origin.

In one case, police in Germany found a murder victim near the Danube River. At that spot the soil contained special fossilized pollen grains found nowhere else. In a city far from the crime scene, police caught a suspect. They were able to link him to the murder scene on the Danube River by examining the mud on his shoes — it contained that rare fossilized pollen!

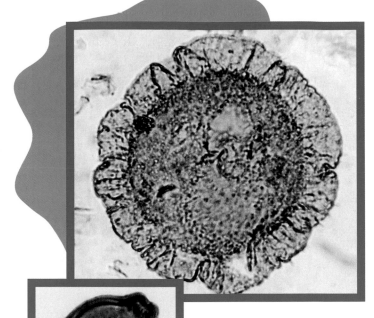

These magnified pictures of pollen show that different kinds have distinctive shapes.

Frosty Ferns

An important piece of evidence — the suitcase of a missing girl — was found on a patch of frosty ground. By the time the forensic botanist got to the scene, fern fronds around the suitcase had melted and turned brown, but ferns underneath it were green. The suitcase had been there since before the frost, and had protected the ferns from the cold.

Flowers on the Grave

It's important that investigators not touch or move anything before it can be studied. A forensic botanist has to be able to check out the plant life at a crime scene before evidence is destroyed. It was fall when police were called in on a case involving a body found under some bushes in a park. They needed to know how long the body had been there.

The forensic botanist identified the bushes as ocean spray. When he examined samples, he found lots of ocean spray pollen on top of the body, but only a little pollen underneath. Pollen from one year usually decomposes before the next year, so the botanist decided that the body must have been placed at that spot just after the ocean spray bushes began to flower that year, but long before they finished (because most of the pollen had fallen on top of the body). He checked the records and found out that ocean spray bushes in that area flowered in the middle of June. He was able to tell police that the body was placed under the bushes in early June.

Digging for Clues

irt can be full of clues. A trained eye can find all sorts of clues underfoot. But you have to dig carefully, or important information will be lost. You need to work like an archeologist unearthing an ancient Egyptian tomb, or a paleontologist uncovering rare dinosaur fossils — bit by bit and with the lightest of touches.

Everything in Its Place

You are uncovering buried bones. The bones themselves are evidence, but they tell only part of the story. Valuable clues can be found by examining how the bones were arranged. On their front? Their back? In a natural pose? Out of order?

Clues can be lost when inexperienced people just collect the bones and send them to the laboratory. The bones should be examined *in situ* (where they were found).

For example, among the bones of a skeleton, police found a bullet and the tattered remnants of a bandanna. Was the bullet in the victim's heart, and therefore the likely cause of death? Or was the bullet sitting in the victim's pocket? Was the victim blindfolded with the bandanna or wearing the bandanna around his head?

What other clues can be found underground? Undisturbed soil has natural layers. If the layering pattern is disturbed, that's a clue that someone has been digging and turning over chunks of soil. An underground sleuth might also find roots that have been cut during the digging. There might be marks from a shovel used to dig a grave. There might even be footprints that were made on the bottom of a grave before it was filled in.

The Real Dirt

Dirt can be a clue to link a suspect to a crime scene. Some dirt is sandy, while some is more like clay. To identify or match dirt samples, forensic geologists look at the color and texture of the soil. Then they wash the soil and look closely at the individual crystals. They shave bits of rock into slices as thin as one-third of a millimetre, so they can be studied under a microscope. Special machines can find out the chemicals in individual grains of sand.

Clues in the Mud

A Pennsylvania man didn't show up at work one morning. Police found his car in the next state, Virginia. They suspected a murder, but couldn't find the body. The police geologist found a build-up of mud on the car. The mud was not made up of layers from different places. The mud got on the car when the driver stepped on the gas and spun the tires in the mud, maybe after the body was dumped.

Looking through crystals from the mud, the geologist found microscopic bits of white and yellow reflective paint, the kind used to paint lines on the side of a road at a hill or curve. There were also bits of black slag — rock left over from iron smelting. Slag was used in Pennsylvania to make anti-skid pavement. Finally, the geologist found microscopic fossils from a type of limestone found at the earth's surface in only two places — one in Pennsylvania. There was only one road crossing that area of Pennsylvania limestone.

The geologist told the police to drive along that road. They should look for an uphill curve with yellow and white painted lines along the side of the road. They should look a short distance down the slope beside the road.

The next day the police called back. "We got the body," they said. "It was there, under a pile of brush."

Watery Evidence

Not all water is the same — especially under a microscope. Water from different places contains different chemicals and microscopic organisms. Police can compare two water samples (say, the water where a body was dumped in the river and water from wet socks a murder suspect was wearing) and tell whether the samples come from the same source.

Maggots Under the Microscope

D id you know that maggots can help the police solve crimes? When police want to know when a death occurred, and the body has been dead for more than a few days, they call in a forensic entomologist. A forensic entomologist studies the insects that live on a dead body.

Evidence on the Wing

What happens if you leave a piece of meat on the kitchen table? It doesn't take long before flies land on it. A dead body also attracts flies. The first arrive within 24 hours, and sometimes in minutes. These flies are choosing a place to lay their eggs where their larvae (young flies) will have food. Different kinds of flies arrive at different times as the body cools and decomposes. Some won't arrive until the body has been dead for several months.

A fly goes through several stages during its life. Forensic entomologists examine the insects on the corpse to identify the species and the stage of their life cycle. For example, empty pupal cases show that a fly has gone through a complete life cycle on the body. Clues like this help entomologists figure out exactly how long the body has been dead.

There are many things forensic entomologists have to take into account. Each kind of insect has its own life cycle, and reaches stages of growth at a different time or even in a different season. Insects are cold-blooded, so everything slows down in cold weather. It's enough to drive an investigator buggy!

Life cycle of a fly

1. Adult flies lay eggs.

2. The eggs hatch and the larvae (maggots) emerge.

3. The larvae are ready to pupate. They develop a hard outer shell called a pupal case.

4. Adult flies emerge from the pupal cases to start the cycle again.

Nailing Poachers

Insect evidence can help catch poachers. Poachers hunt animals illegally — either by hunting in the wrong season, or by killing animals that are not supposed to be killed. Sometimes they take only part of an animal, like bear paws or mountain sheep antlers, and they leave the rest. A forensic entomologist can establish the time of the kill. Police can tell if the killing was illegal, and can find out who was in the area at the time. Using insect evidence, the police can identify the time of death even after months or years.

Timing Is Everything

When a body has been dead for a short time, other ways are used to determine the time of death:

Body temperature: The body cools at a rate of about 1 degree Celsius (about 2 degrees Fahrenheit) per hour.

Rigor mortis: A few hours after death, the muscles of the body start to tighten. By 8 to 12 hours after death the body is stiff. About 24 hours later, the muscles relax and the body becomes limp.

Lividity (purple marks on the skin): When the heart stops pumping blood through the body, the blood settles to the lowest parts of the body. After about eight hours the pooled blood creates purplish marks on the skin that don't go away.

Fly-Witnesses

For hundreds of years, the only sure evidence to a crime was an eyewitness. This case shows that when eyewitness testimony conflicts, it's forensic science to the rescue. On May 15, 1992, two women were found shot dead. It seemed like a simple case. Witnesses had seen the shooting take place on May 3. Based on that sighting, the police had built up a good case against their suspect.

But other witnesses came forward saying they thought they had seen the two women alive on May 9. If it was true, the earlier eyewitness testimony must be false. The police needed to know the date of the deaths. Was it on May 3 or was it sometime after May 9?

On May 17, a forensic entomologist examined the insects on the bodies. She found that the flies that had landed on the body had laid eggs there. The maggots that had hatched from the eggs had reached a stage that she knew would take at least nine days at normal spring temperatures. The forensic entomologist was able to say that the time of death was sometime before May 6.

With that information in hand, the police knew that the second witnesses were mistaken. The entomologist's evidence supported the story of the eyewitnesses who actually saw the shooting. The police had the right suspect, and the killer was convicted.

CLUE IN

A bear carcass has been found in the woods. Wildlife officials suspect that it was killed illegally, before hunting season opened 30 days ago. Has a crime been committed? That's where you come in. As a forensic entomologist, you have been asked to figure out how long the bear has been dead.

The bear carcass has been left where it was found, and has not been touched. You take a good look, and enter these notes in your notebook:

The carcass was found in a shady spot.

The average daily temperature was 23 degrees Celsius (76 degrees Fahrenheit).

The insects found on the body included the following:

Blowflies (*Calliphora vicina*) – Stage: empty pupal cases found

Cheeseskippers (*Piophilidae* sp.) – Stage: larvae found on fatty tissues

Not found: Lesser house flies (*Fannidae* sp.)

The chart below shows when the larvae of cheeseskippers and lesser house flies will show up on a carcass. It also shows the time it takes for a blowfly to complete one whole life cycle (remember, you found empty pupal cases; see page 58). All times are based on the average daily temperature you noted.

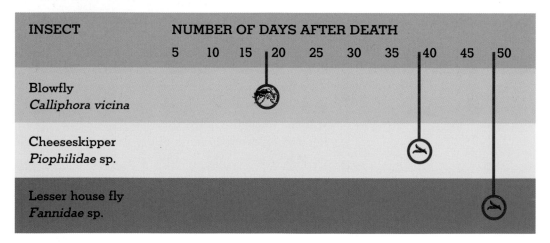

INSECT	NUMBER OF DAYS AFTER DEATH									
	5	10	15	20	25	30	35	40	45	50
Blowfly *Calliphora vicina*				18						
Cheeseskipper *Piophilidae* sp.								40		
Lesser house fly *Fannidae* sp.										50

Was the bear killed during hunting season, or was it hunted illegally? (Answer on page 61.)

Answers

The Case of the Smoking Thief, page 5

Copies of the forensic artist's sketch were distributed to police stations in the area. One officer thought it looked like a thief she had once pulled in for questioning, Tony De Soula. De Soula denied he had anything to do with the robbery. Searching De Soula's car, police found brown fibers that matched the ones found at the bank, but the fibers weren't unusual so they didn't prove anything. While questioning De Soula in his apartment, an investigator found ripped up checks identical to the one used during the holdup. De Soula suggested that someone visiting his apartment might have thrown them in his trash can. The police tested them for fingerprints, but couldn't get a clear enough print.

Finally, police obtained a DNA sample from De Soula. It matched the DNA from saliva on the cigarette butt. With this evidence, plus eyewitness accounts, police arrested De Soula and charged him with armed robbery. The gun and the money were never found.

The Case of the Cyberspace Crook, page 6

To track down the computer thief, the police had computer experts monitor the activity on the university's computer system. Two days later, someone used the professor's password to log in to her account. The experts traced the activity back to the office of Dr. Jerry Small, a physics professor at the University of Othertown. Small was on holiday hiking in the Rockies. Small wasn't a paleontologist, and had no motive for stealing the files. Someone else must have used his computer.

According to the professor, her only competition at the University of Othertown was Dr. Sandra O'Connor. Fingerprints lifted from Small's computer mouse matched O'Connor's, and a witness remembered seeing O'Connor come out of Small's office on the night the professor's files were erased. The evidence strongly implicated O'Connor, but she denied knowledge of the files, and her husband swore she had been home that night. Since the case couldn't be proven, O'Connor was not charged.

The Case of the Mysterious Bones, page 6

At the morgue, a count of the bones showed that they made up only part of a human skeleton. The police looked at the photos of the crime scene to see where the rest of the bones might be. They noticed a place where the soil had been disturbed and plant roots showed fresh cuts. The dirt collected from that area had been freshly dug. They returned to the crime scene and started digging at that spot. They found more bones and the skull, including the teeth, buried in a pit there. They also found prints of a man's workboot in the soil of the pit. Another mystery: the body had been dead a while, since only bones were left, but these bones had been buried in the last few days. Investigators figured that the murderer must have recently returned to where he had hidden the body and found that animals had disturbed it. He must have gathered all the bones he could find and buried them again.

The forensic entomologist could tell from the larvae on the remains that eight to ten months had passed since the time of death. On the rib bones, the anthropologist found marks that looked like knife stab wounds — the cause of death. He estimated the victim was about 167 centimetres (5 feet 6 inches) tall. A forensic dentist determined the victim was male, between 50 and 60 years of age and likely of Asian ancestry. She noticed gold fillings and expensive dental work that suggested the victim was not poor. Working from this descripton, police searched their missing-person files and found a record of a businessman named Lee Chueng reported missing nine months earlier. The forensic dentist made a positive identification by matching Chueng's dental x-rays to the victim's dental chart. Chueng's family was informed, so that they finally knew what had happened to Chueng.

Among the people Chueng had been seen with before he disappeared was San Nguyen, who lived near the spot where the body was found. He owed Chueng thousands of dollars at the time of Chueng's disappearance. Police searched Nguyen's house. In the closet they found workboots that matched the prints found at the crime scene. In a drawer they found a watch and a ring that Chueng's wife identified as belonging to her husband. Behind the house they found a shovel, and the clay soil stuck to it was similar to the soil near the crime scene. When Nguyen was arrested and presented with this evidence, he admitted he had killed Chueng.

Clue In, page 11

The mold of suspect Y's teeth matches the bite mark on the cup.

Clue In, page 23

The forgery is sample C.

Clue In, page 27

The following words can be found in a very complete dictionary: zemindar, varactor, exegesis and xanthoma. Therefore, the made-up passwords are baifudir, prolteif, crutnopa and geroleis.

Clue In, page 43

Lane 5 shows the results of DNA tests on the blood stain from the victim's apartment. The blood stain contains DNA that matches both the victim's blood and the suspect's, so they both must have bled there. If the suspect was the thief, he would have been involved in the scuffle and bled from the wounds he received. The results shown in lane 6 confirm these suspicions — the stain on the suspect's clothes is a DNA match with the blood sample from the victim. The victim's blood on the suspect's clothes proves he was the one the victim fought off, and therefore is the thief. The suspect is lying.

Clue In, page 49

The x-ray is from the body of Ms. Gold.

Clue In, page 60

The bear must have been dead at least 39 days, but not more than 48 days. Here's why:

Cheeseskipper (*Piophilidae* sp.) larvae were found. The chart shows that these larvae aren't found on a carcass until about 39 days after death. Lesser house fly (*Fannidae* sp.) larvae were not found. These insects arrive later than cheeseskippers. According to the chart, their larvae are found on a carcass 48 – 50 days after death. Therefore, the bear must have been dead at least 39 days but not more than 48. That means that it was killed before hunting season opened.

What about the blowflies? These insects are among the first to arrive and lay eggs on a dead animal. The fact that empty blowfly pupal cases were found means that the bear had been dead at least 18 days. The chart shows that 18 days is the time it takes for one full blowfly life cycle — eggs to larvae to pupae to hatched adults — at that temperature. But you already know the bear has been dead longer than that because of the cheeseskippers.

CriMe ScienTists

The police investigate, and forensic scientists use their expertise to help solve the crimes. What a team! When the experts in the lab lend a hand to the law, criminals hardly stand a chance.

In the Lab

Forensic **anthropologists** specialize in bones. They are experts at digging them up, identifying them and analyzing them for clues. In cases where identifying the remains of a victim is the first step to solving the crime, forensic anthropologists are essential — no bones about it!

Forensic **biologists** work with body substances, such as blood, DNA or saliva. These experts mix and match, identifying what substances come from which bodies, living or dead. One type of forensic biologist is a **DNA specialist**, who works at a police forensic lab, identifying and comparing DNA samples.

Forensic **botanists** get to the root of the matter — and the stem, leaves and pollen of the matter, too. Plants growing at the scene of a crime can provide clues about when or where the crime took place. Microscopic parts of plants, such as pollen grains, can sometimes link a suspect to a crime scene. A forensic **dendrologist** is a botanist specializing in wood. Dendrologists can get a lot of information about the timing of a crime by examining wood grain and tree growth rings.

Forensic **chemists** find the right stuff. They figure out what substances are made of, or compare two substances to see if they have the same chemical make-up. The stuff they study can be paint, ink, cloth fibers, blood, stains — almost anything.

Forensic **dentists** (or **odontologists**) really sink their teeth into their work. They identify people and discover important clues by checking out teeth and bite marks.

Entomologists study insects, so it makes sense that forensic **entomologists** are buggy for insects found at crime scenes or on dead bodies. When forensic entomologists gather insects in jars, their bug collections help them discover circumstances of the crime, including the time of death.

The **manager of the forensic laboratory** is the member of the police force in charge of the scientific lab where evidence is analyzed by experts in forensic science.

Forensic **geologists** dig soil and rocks. They have the dirt on what kind of rocks or mud come from where, and know when somebody has been digging and disturbing the natural layers in the soil.

Forensic **pathologists** are doctors who examine dead bodies for clues about the crime.

Forensic **physicists** combine the law and the laws of physics. They're good at figuring out how things happened, like how blood spattered in a particular pattern, or how fast a bullet was shot.

The Long Arm of the Law

Forensic **artists** draw criminals or victims so that others can identify them. Using descriptions given by witnesses, or an unidentified skull, they can construct a face. They also use computer programs to alter photographs and make people look older or younger.

Police **computer crime specialists** investigate crimes in cyberspace.

Computer systems managers set up and run computer networks. A police **computer systems manager** helps the police use computers to speed up criminal investigations.

A police **coroner** coordinates crime investigations involving dead bodies, calling in the forensic experts required, and pulling together all the pieces of information they collect.

Handwriting analysts examine all kinds of written documents. They are handy at spotting forgeries and alterations.

The police **identification officer** is the first in line to be called to the crime scene. Identification officers take photographs and measurements, dust for fingerprints, look for clues, send evidence to the crime lab for analysis, talk to witnesses and often even solve the crime.

The police **inspector** is in charge of all ongoing investigations. The inspector has to know about all areas of forensic science.

Got a voice and you don't know whose? Call a forensic **voice identification specialist** who researches ways to identify individuals from their speech patterns.

Author's Acknowledgements

When I started working on this book, I knew absolutely nothing about forensic science. Luckily, I knew how to ask questions. Many police and forensic experts took the time to help me learn about their work. Thanks to them all!

Gail Anderson, forensic entomologist; Barry Beyerstein, handwriting analyst; John Bowen, DNA specialist; Kevin Bowers, computer systems manager; Custom Cheques of Canada (for anti-counterfeiting features in checks); Leigh Dillon, forensic entomologist; Doug Dzurko, police computer crime specialist; Robert Grant, police computer systems manager; Laurel Gray, pathologist; Richard Hebda, forensic botanist; L.A. Josza, forensic dendrologist; Rick Klevans, forensic voice identification specialist; Rolf Mathewes, forensic botanist; Gordon Meisner, police identification officer; Chico Newell, police coroner; Shawn Odette, Royal Bank; Cam Pye, forensic artist; Kathy Reichs, forensic anthropologist; Mark Skinner, forensic anthropologist; Brian Strongman, police inspector (I had him read this book to make sure I didn't include any mistakes, although I may have snuck in a few later); David Sweet, forensic dentist/odontologist; Dennis Thrift, police forensic laboratory manager; Peter Wood, entomologist.

IndEx